a woman is a woman

is a woman is a woman

poems by Chrys Tobey

a woman is a

a woman is a woman is a woman is a woman is a
woman is a woman is a woman is a woman is a woman
is a woman is a woman is a woman is a woman is a
woman is a woman is a woman is a woman is a woman
is a woman is a woman is a woman is a woman is a
woman is a woman is a woman is a woman is a woman
is a woman is a woman is a woman is a woman is a
woman is a woman is a woman is a woman is a woman
is a woman is a woman is a woman is a woman is a
woman is a woman is a woman is a woman is a woman
is a woman is a woman is a woman is a woman is a
woman is a woman is a woman is a woman is a woman
is a woman is a woman is a woman is a woman is a
woman is a woman is a woman is a woman is a woman
is a woman is a woman is a woman is a woman is a
woman is a woman is a woman is a woman is a woman
is a woman is a woman is a woman is a woman is
woman is a woman is a woman is a woman is a woman

poems **Chrys Tobey**

STEEL TOE BOOKS BOWLING GREEN, KENTUCKY

ISBN: 978-0-9863575-2-7

STEEL TOE BOOKS
Western Kentucky University
Department of English
1906 College Heights Blvd. #11086
Bowling Green, Kent. 42101-1086

BOOK DESIGNED BY THOM CARAWAY

Steel Toe Books is affiliated with Western Kentucky University

Table of contents

I. Marie Antoinette Dreams of Narwhales

II. Cleopatra Loses a Lemon

III. Ms. Bovary is a Bastard

Acknowledgments

My sincere gratitude to the following journals for publishing, or accepting for future publication, poems from this manuscript:

Atlanta Review: "My Alter Egos Ran Off With This Poem"
Cloudbank: "Elegy for Sleep"
Common Ground Review: "All I Know of Love"
Hawaii Pacific Review: "My Mother was Neptune"
Lilies & Cannonballs Review: "My Mother's Latest Theory"
Margie: "Seven Things I Know About Hearts"
Pearl: "I Want This Poem To"
Pinyon: "For the Billboard Near My Home That Reads *God Forgives Everything*"
Ploughshares: "I Am Pretending There Was No Restaurant"
Poetic Diversity: "For the Men Who Inquire" and "The Stapler"
Portland Review: "One Morning"
Rattle: "The Loss of Lemons"
Rio Grande Review: "How to Love"
Satellite Telephone: "For My Second Husband"
Slab: "Taking Care" and "Ms. Bovary Goes House Hunting in 2014"
Smartish Pace: "King Henry (VIII) in the 21st Century," "Lub Dub," and "Dear Monday"
The Cincinnati Review: "So Far, It Looks Like I May Live a Long Life"
The Great American Poetry Show: "The Loss of Lemons" (reprinted)
the minnesota review: "The 260-Pound Zeus"
The Mochila Review: "Headaches"
The Nervous Breakdown: "Narwhals"
Third Wednesday: "Nevermore"
Two Hawks Quarterly: "Headaches" (reprinted) and "Seven Things I Know About Hearts" (reprinted)
Verdad: "Fevers"

Word Riot: "For the Guy Who Unfriended Me on Facebook after I Got Married"

"Seven Things I Know About Hearts" received Semi-Finalist for *Margie's* Marjorie J Wilson Award for 2006. *Smartish Pace* nominated "Dear Monday" for Pushcart Prize 2016.

"18th Century Gossip," "Actresses," "Marie Antoinette Visits the Moon," "Marie Antoinette & Sylvia Plath Go for Ice Cream," and "Off With Marie's Head" are from my chapbook *Wash Away: Marie Antoinette Visits My Mind,* published by Finishing Line Press.

Gratitude to Poetry Press Week for featuring some of the poems from this manuscript during their Spring/Summer 2014 show.

The poems in this book span some time, and I'm truly grateful to some of the most generous and talented humans who have given support, feedback and encouragement throughout the making of this manuscript. I may be forgetting someone and if I am, know you are deep in the bowels of my heart (though I'm not sure you want to be there). Thank you Frank X. Gaspar, Carol Potter, Jenny Factor and Eloise Klein Healy, for the inspiration, for being my teachers whom I continue to learn from. Thank you Richard Garcia, for so much, but most of all, for being my mentor in the truest sense of the word. Thank you Peter Sears, for your sheer kindness and advice. Thank you Steel Toe Books for selecting this manuscript and to Tom C. Hunley, for your humor and guidance. Thank you Nikia Chaney, fellow Boob Poet; Carl Adamshick, for being the Big C; Donald Strauss, for your years of kindred encouragement. Thank you Tammy Lynne Stoner, for your endless support, for being my A.S.S. I am beholden to the following women who are so insanely generous, they defy a human's capacity for generosity—Armine Iknadossian and Jennifer Bradpiece, for all the feedback, for the enthusiasm, for the friendship; this manuscript would not be possible without your brilliant brains and your love. Thank you Justin Rigamonti, for the hours upon hours upon hours of scrutinizing individual poems and the manuscript, for your insight, for your sassy b**&# camaraderie (you can have my liver, but you probably don't want it). Of course, thank you Allison Tobey—my sister—who patiently helped me with all of this and whom all of this is for. And, lastly, thank you Nate Szytel, for the left side of your brain, for the right side of your brain, and for your heart.

This book is also dedicated to Moe Powers (1923—2002), who gave me my first book of poetry.

For Allison

****

Does she have a pleasing telephone personality?
—Susan Griffin

1

Marie Antoinette Dreams of Narwhales

Where Were We?

Oh yes, we were talking about how the world is ending—
In less than fifty years all the fish will be gone you say,
the fish, you keep repeating, *the fish,* as if they are your last hope,
as if you've been floating with the waves, witnessing
their translucence travel past you and someone just scooped
you out with a net. We've been talking about this twice a week
for years now—this ending—as we drive from work, and I think:
if this is it, if this is all we have left, let us pull into the nearest
motel parking lot—dimly lit and not a car in sight—let us rent a room
with an analogue TV and the smell of bleach, let us tear down
these years of longing—these years of *what if,* these years of others
lying in the sanctity of our sleep—with our teeth. Let our legs
tremble. Let our hands clasp wrists. Let our lips open to taste
salt of skin. Let us fuck and fuck and fuck until our heat
warms this record low Oregon night. Let us fuck and fuck
until we give the animals in the Arctic back their ice. Let us
pull hair and scream until our bodies stick to sweaty sheets. Let our
stomachs rise. Let us do this again and again and again until we feed
your beautiful fish, until the ocean is full of their orange scales and gray fins.
But—we're still driving. My lumbar is hurting and we passed
the last motel going 70 mph. We're sick with hunger and silence
and then you ask, *Do you really think this is the end?* And I sigh, *No, not yet.*

Narwhals

When I was ten, my mother sat me down
and told me my real father was a narwhal.
My report cards always read, *Daydreams too much.*
What my teachers did not know is that I was busy
dreaming about eating a grilled cheese sandwich
with a narwhal or how all 4,000 pounds
of my narwhal father was going to sit
on the kids who threw rocks the size of houses
at my head. How he was going to stick
his overgrown tooth in Robby's eye for stealing
carved pumpkins from my back porch.
How he was going to submerge like a submarine
when large Lisa Dooley challenged
me to meet her behind the janitor's tool shed.
My mother thought I was slow, which
was fine because I loved Peewee Herman.
Doctors looked inside my head, but all they could ever
see were narwhals fencing with their tusks
off the coast of Russia, or catching some cod.

Elegy for Sleep

You are the salty skin
of my childhood love slipping
out my bedroom window,
the eggs my mother fries
before she leaves for her night shift,
the creak of my father's footsteps.
Sleep, without you, my mind
is a car door slammed hard,
my eyes, two wet towels,
my mouth, a rope
words cannot walk straight on.
Sleep, meet me
on the flight to Paris.
Meet me on the Santa Monica beach,
sand sliding between my toes.
Meet me on the train to Seattle,
in the stiff sheets of the hotel room in Victoria,
my old stucco apartment, this wood floor.
I won't talk about the time
I went without you for five days.
Won't bring up Lunesta or Ambien.
Won't drink too many margaritas—
you can lick the salt from my lips.
I'll bathe myself in chamomile
and spread lavender lotion on my legs.
Sleep, seduce me: whisper in my ear.
Slide my face into this pillow.
Squeeze my wrists and tell me
I'm going nowhere. Tell me
I'll obey you. Tell me
I've got something coming.

Lub Dub

Piñata Heart. Heart of a thousand crunchy candies.
No heart of gold heart. LA's honking horns heart.
Never left my arteries in San Francisco heart.
Heart of mud and sticks. Oh heart, break my bones.
Arthritic hand of a heart. Unfold your fingers.
Too many fathers in my heart. Too many tiny
metal balloons in one father's heart.
Carry the groceries heart. *I'll carry*
the bag with lettuce and fish heart.
Is this umbrella hurting your arm heart.
No lub dub on my sleeve heart.
Heart on my wing. Bird heart.
Heart of chicken feathers. Chicken heart.
Ferris wheel heart. Get on, get off heart.
Jell-O mush heart. Stop being mush heart.
Straighten up and fly right heart. Fly right, heart.
Fly right out of this coop.

King Henry (VIII) in the 21ˢᵗ Century

King Henry counts his lies like he used
to count his mother's cigarettes. His mother
who still says *baby boy* & still makes him eggs
with thick hollandaise, just the way King Henry likes it—
because a woman is a woman is a woman is a woman.
King Henry knows a woman should *not* sit that way.
King Henry knows when his woman *should* sit that way.
King Henry says a woman should have childbearing eyes & lustful thighs
& he knows the art of love: pay her parking tickets
& be the first to marry her & hold her hair back
& say *there, there*. King Henry's right-hand-man shuffles
things out of his mind—like past wives—since King Henry's
mind is two bookends. King Henry buys a BMW.
King Henry tints the windows of his BMW—
because a woman is a woman is a woman is a woman.
Yes, King Henry knows love is nothing more than a game of
musical chairs: he can send one away ~~and~~ & another will take her place.

One Morning

she woke up and couldn't rub penises from her eyes. She was unsure
how this happened. You'd think she was *gettin' around*, as her mother
used to say. But no, she was married to a real, genuine penis. Some
would say a savory penis. But now she saw penises everywhere: She
opened her door to penises promising Jesus. She read magazines
full of penises. She turned on the television to penises. All kinds of
penises—short penises, fat penises, slim penises. Penises planning
infrastructure and coding computers. Brown penises. White penises.
Penises pontificating. Penises invading. Stiff penises interviewed by
important penises about such seriousness—*Well, Charlie, it's not quite a
cold war. I know*—it's hard to imagine. But penises were strung across
her mind like holiday lights. Suddenly she saw penises strumming
guitars. Penises singing about their own penises. Corporate penises.
Elected penises. She was stumped. She went to lunch with a friend
who said *You know, most women would've slept with that penis to get ahead.*
And she thought, *as if a penis were some kind of pole vault. As if you could
climb a penis to the sky.*

Marie Antoinette Visits the Moon

Earth looks like a Christmas ornament
from this giant piece of marble cake.
And for the record—It wasn't *Let them eat cake.*
I said *Boy, would I like a piece of cake.*
But really, none of that matters now.
I would like to have been an astronaut,
like a balloon no one can quite reach.
From here France looks like a scrap
of glitter that could wipe away.
You know, I used to stare at the moon
and wish I could glue a string onto it,
like a kite I'd grab and drift far from Versailles.

Moon

Pardon me, I feel tired and annoyed,
like I've been bleeding for days
and all I want is a good plate of nachos.
So for the next week please stop
projecting your shit onto me—
lonely, wild, upset, longing,
love lost, trying to read my face —
It's the back of my head you're staring at.
I'm the big shrink in the sky and I don't
get paid a buck. Plath was onto something
when she wrote I'm not sweet like Mary.
Yes, I feel some empathy for Plath—
the way you pick her apart like you're
digging for the chicken in your quesadilla.
This is all I can tell you about love:
you look like shiny silver spoons
staring up at me. I really appreciated
John Lennon's voice, the way he'd sing
I'm just a jealous guy. I'm envious of the sun,
how he gets to see you in all that light.
I could tell you how it sounded
when Sappho played her lyre,
who killed Marilyn, Che Guevara & Jesus,
whether King Louis was gay or straight.
You think God sees everything.
But you'll just keep searching
like a military ship, off the coast
of Columbia, searching for the mother load
in a phantom submarine. I will tell you this:

Elvis is not alive. And Emily Dickinson
had a potty mouth. If I could come down there,
I'd shop the boutiques of Paris with an orange scarf
blowing in the breeze. For the time being, keep howling.
You people are so funny when you howl at me, whisky on your breath.

For the Guy Who Unfriended Me on Facebook After I Got Married

Darling, there were once other ways to go about this —
a letter scribbled with a final *goodbye*—the *e* a hand closing —

stored away in some drawer or box, something I could
open thirty years from now, when I'm considering my regrets.

Or a telephone call—you wouldn't even have to speak; we could
sit in silence, or sigh, until one of us slams down the receiver.

And then, there were more creative ways—once, a past lover
threw eggs at me as I left work, or I saw two men beat each other

like drums until the scream of fire-trucks and ambulances pulled them apart.
When my grandfather remarried, my grandmother sent him one white rose.

Think of all the objections at the altar—you could've been a baritone horn blasting
in the ears of tight-lipped and teary-eyed guests. Oh my dear, we have none of this —

nothing to crumple up, no way to feel the stars burn out in my hands.

Gossip, 18th Century Style

Gambled and drank until dawn,
you know that Austrian whore,
thinks about orgies every time she yawns,
all her lovers, those kids weren't really the King's,
wouldn't give him sex, she'd slam the door.
Wait, didn't she have sex with a horse?
Stole a diamond necklace,
had an affair with Madame La Motte —
Oh the nerve of that Austrian whore.
Her own children hated her,
her dying son wouldn't see her,
for she was no kind of mother,
taught her little boy to masturbate.
Off with the head of that Austrian whore!
You know she was a spy, lies, lies, lies,
let the people starve & die, while she built theaters
and threw operas and balls and parties galore,
poor, poor Louis let her take more and more.
Let them eat cake she screamed.
Oh the nerve of that Austrian whore.

My Mother was Neptune

I'm not sure if she was always a planet
far off in our solar system, farthest from the sun,
made of ice and rock—or if it happened the year
I was born, the year the great blizzard swept through.
Teachers would hang planets from strings, and I'd think,
There's my mother as Neptune hovered over me like a blue eye.
I'd put on my tinfoil spacesuit and eat astronaut ice cream,
or I'd bounce up and down with my astronaut bubblehead.
I carried around a blanket, knowing it was cold
where she was. Sometimes I'd get close
and a cool gust of wind would blow me back.
When I was twelve, scientists sent their spacecraft to her.
As it circled, she simply stared off at her surrounding moons,
remembering how she was once thought to be luminous.

The Closet

A woman remodeled herself into a closet. She liked it this way. People could make good use of her. They stored their old golf clubs and hats inside of her. She was rarely bothered, except for the occasional sweeping.

The woman read love letters as forgotten as old shoes. She paged through porn men hid from their wives. She looked at family photos: birthdays, vacations, first marriages, second marriages, third marriages. The woman thumbed through bank statements, credit card bills, stock accounts each night. This lulled her to sleep. The woman shut her door on husbands' fingers & watched their nails bruise black.

"Ah, this fucking closet," the husbands screamed and kicked the door. The woman smiled and went back to counting silver.

Since You Have Not Responded to My Previous Attempts to Contact You

Dear Sasquatch, I know there are people
obsessed with their headlamps and tents,
and yes, I watched *Harry and the Hendersons*
as a kid—but I've felt you in the morning fog
as my car door creaks open, in the branches brushing
along my skin, the scattering of leaves, and the tapping
on my window as my ex snored me to sleep.
Sasquatch, my heart drops whenever I see a dead deer.
I don't care if you cut your hair into a mullet, or shed all over the couch.
I'll buy a California King; I really don't take up much room.
But, I'm no longer of the age when hope gave me a headache
like new paint. So Sasquatch, this is my last attempt: I will leave
the deadbolt unlocked and a brush by the side of the bed.

For the Billboard Near My Home That Reads *God Forgives Everything*

Dear God, please forgive me for wiping lipstick and snot
all over my ex's passenger seat before I left him. He bought
a new car two days later, but still. Please forgive my sister
for replacing our drunk dad's patchouli with hot sauce. I know
it was technically my sister, but I did egg her on. Can you also forgive
my sister for suffocating me with Dutch ovens, and forgive me
while you're at it because though it was gross, it was still pretty funny.
And, consider forgiving us for laughing at men with perfectly
round rear-ends, or *bubble butts*, unfortunate when they stand in front
of us in lines and I know this plays into gender biases, which you probably
don't care about, but you probably do care about the laughing.
Dear God, my dog keeps pissing in my closet and I fear
I'm walking around in clothes that smell of urine, and if I am,
please forgive me. Dear God, please forgive my potty humor—
my mother says it's not right—and how I burp in front
of my husband, usually after a meal, when I'm well aware
he cannot burp for some medical reason. Dear God, forgive me
for smirking every time I hear your name, but you could've
gone with something a bit more pretentious—like Godidiah—
since the scientists say we should name something
with more than one syllable if we want it to respond.

Taking Care

A woman wasn't sure where to take Care. She thought perhaps Care would like to visit the ocean. The woman buckled up Care in a maroon minivan and drove to the Pacific. The ocean cradled them like a blue rocking chair. The blue rocking chair broke, and crashed down onto them. So the woman took Care to a park. The woman and Care each sat in a swing. Care would not swing because it reminded her of the ocean. The woman asked, *Care, where should I take you?* Care casually said, *The moon.*

The woman took Care to the moon. The moon reminded Care of the ocean, its craters like imprints of sand. Care wanted to leave. The woman looked down from the moon: she could see Ohio, sitting like a bitten cookie on a tray, where she had grown up. *If only Ohio looked like this up close,* the woman thought. Then she saw California, stretched out like a wet towel. The woman looked closer and saw the white stucco apartment she once lived in. And there he was: her husband standing outside of the screen door, his cobalt eyes looking up at the moon. The woman scooped Care up, the way a spoon would scoop ice cream, threw Care from the moon, and yelled down to her husband the last thing he had said to her—*Take care.*

Cleopatra Loses a Lemon

My Alter Egos Ran Off With This Poem

1. Catherine The Great

I did not roll out of a carpet
like Cleopatra or wait for this crown
like a fatherless child waits by the window.
I accepted my fate the same way
I knew not to get up from breakfast
until I finished my milk. The same way
my mother accepted a legacy
of biting her tongue, her silence the cloak
of silver weighing me down on my wedding day.
This crown was a screaming newborn —
Here, take it, they said, and I did —
its diamonds and pearls still crushing my head.

2. Cleopatra

So I rolled out of a carpet. I know history
loves a good slut, but let me be clear:
it was not to suck Caesar off.
I jumped through a hoop to build
a city of gold, a library as full as a fat man's belly.
I fed mouths, and I knew the world was not flat.
But still, all you can think about is who I gave head.
How I wore too much gold. I was growing old.
Even Catherine The Great had feathers
flying from her bed. But a woman knows
what will bring her power: it's not a night of grunts
and sweat, but a mind sharp enough
to slice through his neck.

3. Marie Antoinette

I wanted my head to be their kickball.
I wanted them to get some use out of it,
like a native people paying homage
to the buffalo they're about to eat.
What a waste—years of learning languages,
words and numbers, little planets in my mind.
How I'd imagine my skirt was a hot air balloon
that would sail me to Saint Petersburg, set me
next to Empress Catherine. How we'd drink
champagne and speak of Voltaire. How we'd
laugh about the first time we tried to have sex
in a place as foreign as the moon
with boys available as the night sky.
How I envy her—a woman who never
had to smell the executioner's sour breath,
never had to watch his trembling hand.

The Loss of Lemons

A woman had lemons in her head. She could feel them the same way she could feel a star dying. The woman insisted on getting an MRI. She wanted to see X-rays of the lemons. She imagined it would be like looking at the moon suspended in the night sky. The technician gave her Bocelli to listen to. The woman smiled as the conveyer belt slid her into the machine like luggage in an airport.

The woman had no idea what Bocelli was singing. *Estoy muriendo amor porque te extraño.* She imagined the words were something about lemons. *Te extraño, te extraño.* Perhaps he had lost lemons. The conveyer belt shook back and forth, jiggled her body, as though she were on a motorboat. *Te extraño, te extraño.* Then the woman saw it: the ferry motoring towards Capri. She looked closer and saw her husband. The woman looked closer still and saw her husband smiling, his one missing tooth, on a tiny bus winding its way up the roads of Capri. And then she smelled the lemons. She saw the lemon orchards, lemon trees stretching for miles, wrapping around Capri like the gold ring that once wrapped around her finger.

The Stapler

is weeping, the calendar is asleep
and the scissors yell *shut the fuck up.*
The stapler whispers *I'm lonelier than the moon*
and the checkbook cackles with laughter.
The flowered picture frame says
Hey, you want to talk about lonely
as the computer stares in disbelief,
and the purple desk lamp thinks it's raining.
The stapler glances over at the picture frame,
starts to say something but the stack
of blank journals curses and screams.
The empty camera case starts singing
You're once, twice, three times a lady...
and the phone book sneezes
and the unused day planner says
Look, at least you're married
and the stapler weeps and weeps.

For the Men Who Inquire

You ask where my husband is,
the faceless man we must paint a face onto.
We must give him an occupation,
preferably no better than yours.

A starched ivory shirt, maybe I starched
and ironed the shirt (am I that kind of wife?),
beige slacks that hang loose around his crotch,
not too loose, his cock may be no larger than yours.

Black stones where the eyes are placed,
gaping holes for teeth, and of course a bald head.
A name? Shall we give him a name?
No, no name—*The Husband* will do.

Dear, you ask where my husband is.
Shall I pull him from my pink purse,
tug my ear, carve him from the wall,
or maybe I'll spread my pale legs and he'll crawl out.

My Mother's Latest Theory

It was that rat.
She has never told anyone this
and she sounds like a priest
who has finally spoken.
That old rented house,
in a large field, with long strands of grass, like hair,
a house hidden behind a Bob Evans.
She saw this rat at the top of the wooden stairs,
next to my room, in its casual brown suit.
She confesses how it would squeeze beneath
my bedroom door and gnaw its way into my crib.
The rat is responsible.

The 260-Pound Zeus

His chariot: a 1970s brown Buick station wagon
with a busted back window and a screwdriver
to start the ignition. A tank.
It could travel by water. It could travel by land.
Rolling Rock bottles from the passenger side
would clink together, little bells from above,
as he turned into the driveway.
A twenty-four pack his shield, my father revealed
himself, god of sky, god of everything that falls—
chipped mugs, blue benches, forks, knives, checkbooks—
striking walls, floors, sometimes my mother
as her eyes turned into avalanches—
he once turned her into a sphinx
for silencing his nymphs.
He once took away her mouth.
Her hands became fins as she sat
gluing a fallen footstool back together—
he roared *Fuck you! Fuck you! Fuck you!*
Shaking his shield as my sister's piggy bank spiraled
down the stairs, hailing nickels, pennies, dollar bills.
His footsteps booming, rocking the house,
rattling the cupboards, as the wind turned
into his cigarette smoke coiling
around my ears, as I collected his thunderbolts
and stored them in my closet.

Headaches

Sour milk down the throat,
seagulls screeching in your ear,
tearing your mind in half like sour dough.
You're trapped in an elevator.
Someone is peeling off your pinky nails.
Your neighbor drills holes into your clock.
You've got needles in your gums.
Your eyeballs have no sockets,
smell of rotting tooth, singed skin.
The doctor cauterizes your nose,
bathes you in cheap cologne.
Helicopters circle around your head.
Both legs fall asleep.
The lobster is a raw onion.
The child cries in a pot.
Your head is a jammed printer,
a heart pumping
through your temples
—*lub dub, lub dub*—
cracked asphalt.
You've got two craters on the moon.
Your eyes are flashlights.
You dive into a bathtub,
walk on warm sand,
step on a rusty nail.
You're the car door
your thumb is stuck in.

For the Guy From My Yoga Class Who Asked If He Could Urinate On My Face

Oh Holy Grail of urine. Oh fountain of flushed and soft skin.
Wash away my sins, my years of longing, my years of wanting
too much. Oh blessed piss, cleanse my mind. Oh golden
stream, give me purity. Give me peace. Give me back my
youth with your geyser of sweet, sweet pee. Give me back hope.
Oh pink pipe of piss, wash away these lines. Wash away my
cynicism. Let your urine cascade down my temples for days.
Let it turn my hair yellow again. Let it wash away these aches.
Let my face be your ravine. Let rivulets of your pee run down
my cheeks. Oh smell of sour ammonia, bless me with happiness.
Whatever this means, give it to me. Oh guy of a million downward
dogs, guy with the heavenly spout, anoint me with your naiveté,
anoint me with the assumption that I can just piss on anyone.

How to Love

First, you must not approach this like a scientist
who studies the social interactions of ants.
Now, you will want to find a young thing.
Her lips should be a red ribbon you can pull.
Do not tell her you want to be bent over her knee.
Now and then, draw a bath for her tired feet and buy her a cat
if she wants a cat and if she does not want a cat, buy one anyway.
When her mind becomes a sailor sick for land, take her to Paris.
Call her mother at least once a month, but whatever you do,
do not tell her mother you've been visiting the S & M parlor
where a hooker bends you over her knee.
When her throat is a spiral staircase, buy her crab legs.
If she's too rough with garments, hand-wash her underwear.
Don't tell her how the black lace callousing your hands
makes you think how you want her bent over the hooker's knee.
On Sundays, walk with her to her favorite café where she will
eat a chocolate crepe and drink a frothy latte.
And, because this is love, she will leave.
After she leaves, take up the study of ants
and how they wage wars.

I Want This Poem To

Stain your nails yellow,
ooze out with each lie—
I just couldn't make it work anymore.
I want you to see this poem
in the steam of your shower door.
The silence between
How are you? and *Good.*
Each car horn, baby's cry,
in the stamp that punches
your stock market tickets,
the black in your fourth cup of coffee,
the garlic in your chicken parmesan
and the fork scraping the plate clean.
I want each word to coil around
your neck like blue smoke
in the bar where you meet
your next lover,
each letter sliding
from her tongue
and into your mouth,
slipping between the cracks
of each tooth, filling your gap
like the clump of sauerkraut
you ate in Munich
on our honeymoon.
The green in the bills
you hand her, the clink
of her gold heels
after she quietly closes the door
and walks down the stairs.
The swig of vodka,
the feathers of the pillow

your head falls into.
I want this poem to
curl into your lashes,
and stare you down
like the face of the moon.

Nevermore

Poe believed art should begin at the end, move
the first word to the last: *nevermore.*
A boy outside my window, yellow hair over
one eye, yells *Fuckin' Pussy! Faggot!* He will never
know I am writing him into this poem and I can remove
his words like the fishhook the doctor had to remove
from my father's bottom lip. I'm not sure words are more
than tiny hooks we cast into the air and veer
away from. I think we should be able to move
first words to last: move *love* & *forever.*
Hooks I cannot dig out of my mind, cannot replace or
rid like the yellow haired boy's words, no
Poe's trick of the pen. No childhood game of Red Rover.
You can't remove a word from a word, a nerve
from a piece of fish, *never* from *nevermore.*

For My Second Husband

You are like trying to clutch steam
or like doggy paddling through air.

Though my husband is certain of you.
Your second husband won't love you like I do, he says.

Honestly, I've barely thought of you—
like a god I'm not quite sure exists.

Your second husband will never know you
like I do, my husband says.

He speaks as though he can see you
waiting in your car, engine running.

You're like struggling to spot plasma
in a candle flame or like a still fly a frog can't find.

You'll never go through as much with him
as you have with me, my husband says.

Who are you? It's as though you're lightning
my husband spots long before I hear the thunder.

Perhaps I'll return to my childhood love.
Many people do, yearning to feel known.

Though my childhood love wouldn't recognize me,
like a rural area developed into a city.

He will never understand you, my husband says.
Perhaps you won't, my second husband, my City of Z.

awomanisawomanisawomanisawoman///46

Seven Things I Know About Hearts

The heart is the size of a fist and weighs
somewhere near twelve ounces or one pound.

You sent a card that read *A light heart lives long*
for my eighteenth birthday and now I ask
how heavy is the heart that leaves his child?

At birth my heart was the size of a coin
and weighed about two-thirds of an ounce.

It takes sixteen weeks to see the heart,
around the time you pressed for mine to stop.

The woman you fucked as I slipped out must
have had pink nipples the size of my heart.

Aristotle believed that the heart was
the seat of the soul and the center of man.

My heart is a freight train hauling a steel beam.

Catherine The Great Addresses the Audience's Concerns

Dear fools, dear circus monkeys, trained to dismiss,
trained to ridicule. Give me your top hats. Give me
your gossip. I'm no victim of your virtue, of your
moral mush. *She had young lovers! She loved sex!*
you've spat through the centuries. *She tried to have sex
with a horse!* Nope, it was a whale. How dare a woman
have a libido. How dare a woman fuck a man younger
than she. No, we don't have thousands of years
of thousands of men screwing even a flea, thousands
of years of letting their lovers' heads roll
like dice, but we simply say they're totalitarian,
tyrannical, oh, and entertaining. But a woman—
a woman with power—is different, something to defame.
Never mind the many languages she spoke; never mind
her love of reading, writing, Enlightenment and philosophy;
never mind her friendship with Voltaire; never mind her coup;
never mind her husband who was no better than King Henry;
never mind she was a woman who ruled for thirty-eight years, a woman
who did not die by a man. But, I understand your concern, your eagerness
for disregard. Determination *is* dangerous. Ambition
is a threat. Because she may one day write the rules
and then, and then, my saccharine sucklings,
what, oh what, will you do?

Everything You Hate

What would I liked to have been?
Everything you hate.
—The White Stripes

Dogs. A dog clumsy around your feet, begging for your love,
waiting for another crumb, for your hand, for another bone,
dragging my dirt through your home, rolling on the carpet
you can never seem to get clean. Scrub, scrub, I am
a dog and my nails are caked with mud. Toothpaste. I am
stuck to your sink. A wet sponge, a soaking sponge. Squeeze me
hard. Dishes. I am piles of dishes crusted in oatmeal, coated
in oil and butter, smelling of rotting fish. A scratch, a scrape
on your white car. I am a stack of unpaid bills slipping
through your fingers. I am your mother. *Oh baby boy,* I say.
I make any food for you. *Anything you want,* I say. I smother
you with my sorrow for driving away on a December day,
leaving you when you were ten, for another man. I am
the other man. I collect women like Native American art.
Thoughts of their children stick in my dream catchers. When
my stomach sickens from their sadness, I move on. I am
the ocean. How is it you never learned to swim? Wear
your life jacket in three feet of water all you want. I can still suck
you in. I can still pull you under. I can still spit you out.

Marie Antoinette & Sylvia Plath Go for Ice Cream

I hear they've made a movie about you, Marie.
They made one of me. Some silly blonde
played the role - she couldn't finish
reading my diaries. Poor, poor thing.

Oh hell, I'm played by a giddy blonde.

The crowd always loves a blonde.

Careful Sylvia, the poet writing this is blonde.

Why is she making us get ice cream?
I've never liked ice cream. Sometimes gelato.

You know, I never liked vanilla.
Louis was vanilla, too vanilla.

Well then, what was your lover?

Neapolitan.

Ted was the container after
all the ice cream had been licked clean.

Wait, we're giving the crowd what they want—
two *bitch goddesses* for the taking.

Ms. Bovary is a Bastard

So Far, It Looks Like I May Live a Long Life

Vivas to those who have failed!
—Walt Whitman

Failed first grade. Almost failed ninth. Failed
to show up. Failed to stop smoking weed. Failed to pay
a parking ticket. And then another. And another.
Failed to write letters when we still wrote letters.
Failed a business. Failed to understand poets
fail at business. Failed my savings account.
Failed to wash the worm from the lettuce. Failed
my first marriage. Failed the man I should've
left my first marriage for. Failed love. Again.
And again. Failed my driver's test, three times—
actually, it was my sister, but genetically speaking.
Failed California. Failed Ohio. Failed Oregon.
Failed to close the stupid blinds as I stepped
into the shower this morning. Failed to do the dishes.
Failed to change the oil. Failed to make love
in a houseboat. Failed to realize there would only
be one night with a houseboat and the Pacific
and her face barely visible under the failing moon.

Dear Monday

You're up buying bagels, whistling after swallowing another sip
of coffee, before the rest of us rise. Monday, it's not that I'm tired

of the mouth guard you wear at night or the way your jaw clicks as you chew.
But your straight spine, workouts at noon, & balancing of the budget

have me dreaming of Friday, who writes his number on the outside of my latte
because, yes, he is a barista in his thirties, but he says things like, *You should*

come with me to Spain, and the *0* from his number begins to look like a pillow
I can rest my head on. Friday has bourbon on his breath and each time he laughs

I imagine his teeth biting my thigh. Friday's in no hurry, but he thinks he's falling
in love with me. He says, *Let's go to Seattle.* He says, *Leave Monday behind.*

Ms. Bovary Goes House Hunting in 2014

She was the lover in every novel, the heroine in every play,
the vague she in every volume of poetry.
—Flaubert, from *Madame Bovary*

I don't want to live in the sprawl, somewhere in the stifling
heat of the wide streets; I want to live in this tiny two-bedroom
with the pulse of the city beneath my feet; I want
a sink that works and space for a desk. But a woman should
want bay windows and velvet drapes and material things!
A woman should want a house big enough for little feet.
A woman should honor her mother's words—*We're here to have babies*!
A woman should marry a doctor. A woman should
be a muse. Oh, silly me. But place your finger over
the *m* in *muse* and see what's left, and trace the lineage
of women held hostage by a man's pen, the lineage
of women whose hearts were stilled by booze. No, there will
be no pitter-patter in this room. The backyard is big enough for my dog.
This house may be big enough for my thoughts.

For the Editor Who Accepted a Few of My Poems
and Whom I've Since Been Romanticizing

I know I'm too old for this but we have the Internet which makes
maturity so much harder and so yes I've looked at photos of you
and watched Youtube videos where you give quite impressive
speeches and it's made me think I could fly to you or you could fly
to me and maybe we could be like Edna Millay and George Dillon
except they were both poets and he was much younger and I believe
we're about the same age, so maybe we could be like Emily Dickinson
and her editor, but that wasn't so romantic and then you'd have to correct
everything I write and maybe Emily did sit in her room and dream
of the possibilities but they didn't have things like overnight flights,
though it probably wouldn't be a good idea to hop on a plane since
I am married, but Edna was married, but still. In your photos
I've thought you resemble Johnny Depp, not in *Pirates of the Caribbean*
but Johnny in the '90s , maybe in *Ed Wood*, and speaking of the '90s,
we're both artists and Gen Xers which means you probably like to wear
a good pair of Converse and I've always been a sucker for Converse
but not Peter Gabriel and okay, though you have dark eyes and dark hair
you don't really look like Johnny Depp but I'm just going to pretend
and call you Johnny Jr. from here on out: Johnny Jr., I'm so tired
of thinking about rising water and turning on the television
to animals that won't be around much longer and how the narrator
who sounds like Morgan Freeman or sometimes Alec Baldwin
always discloses this in the very end and I missed an event
where we could've met but I didn't go because Dante needed
someone and I'm no Dante, but if we meet you may very well
sound like you're in *Pirates of the Caribbean* and maybe your
handshake feels like a slippery fish and maybe we'd stand in awkward
silence and we'd just be strangers sick to our stomachs on some turbulent flight.

Off with Marie's Head

A pinprick is worse
than the guillotine.

Imagine a butcher's knife
swiftly cutting a tomato.

The worst part was the cart ride,
like a roller coaster creaking through a funhouse.

I thought I heard my little boy scream.
It was a mad man laughing.

My last thought:
I was dead at fourteen.

I am Pretending There Was No Restaurant

as though the ocean swept it away like a sand dune.
If I pretend there was no restaurant then I never
saw your glossy eyes, where the old man
who'd sit at the counter each day
said, *I can tell he's a pervert. Just look at his eyes.*
But if there was no restaurant then there was no old man
and if I pretend there was no restaurant—two streets away
from your apartment—then you never walked in
one evening, before your baseball game,
sat at the counter and asked, *What's good here?*
If I pretend there was no restaurant
then you never watched me,
the way one mutes their television,
as I told you tortilla soup was good.
You never asked me to refill your ice tea,
never tipped the amount of the check.
No, if I pretend there was no restaurant,
as though somehow a hole just sucked it right up,
then you never came in every Saturday for months
asking, *So when are we going to go out?*
You never waited, like a dog waiting for his bone,
as I paused, pulled you closer,
the way I'd tug the thin string of a kite,
and said *Maybe next time.*
If I pretend there was no restaurant,
then I never said *yes* and each *yes*
that followed unravels like the yarn of an old quilt
and you are just a piece of dust
I rubbed out of my eye
a long time ago.

Fevers

It's like glancing in the rearview mirror only to see
a red suburban coming towards you, as you're stopped on the freeway.
It's those monsters that came along with your childhood fevers
or like scraping your gums with a toothpick.
Like running through a field, barefoot, dandelions everywhere,
feet stained yellow, as you step on a bee.
Your eyes are lightening bugs
or your brain is a piece of orange bubble gum.
It's when you arrive somewhere
and it's no different than the place you've left.
Like waking up in a hospital after you've been revived,
with no idea as to how much time has passed
or when you scream at the top of your lungs,
yet no window will break.
It's saying goodbye to your imaginary friend.
Realizing the boy-next-door never loved you
or the pull of a rip tide, while you try to swim to the side,
not to let your heart pound too hard or swim too hard,
just swim to the side.
It's the dream where you wake up while you're falling
or your heart is a cloud, the kind that looks like cotton pulled apart.

The Ferris Wheel

Yes, it's redundant: the day in and day out,
the dull ache of not letting my fingers unfold,
like a sanitation truck or a contraption scooping dog shit—
Here, you hold the bag, I want to say to the bumper car.
It's the baby's scream and the snot left behind,
the sand forever up my nose, the same guy
with the same stuffed animals yelling,
Step right up folks! The constant crunching
of caramel corn, or popcorn, or whatever corn—
imagine a child chewing behind your head
year after year, the birds shitting on me, smashing into me—
I'm this giant hand in the sky, the last thing they see as they fall.
It's how this roller coaster always has his arms around me
like we're an awkward couple at a middle school dance,
but I can't slap his cheek, can't turn away.
It's an arranged marriage and I just want
to scream, *Let me breathe!* It's how I must
shine and sparkle at night like an 18th Century queen
or Lady Gaga on a world tour. If only I could travel.
If only I could fold up into an airplane. Oh, how
I envy the ocean: she waves her flabby arms at me
and I want to unhinge myself and jump in.
But I stay because of them: who else would remember
the flush of cheeks, palms sweaty, as they rush from
the photo booth, how he scoots closer just to smell
her shampoo, how she says, *I hope you know
I don't kiss on first dates.* How they think it will last.
How they'll split in ten years: he'll go and marry someone else,
she'll move north, and how I'll be the only one left
this means anything to.

She Wears Her Sadness Well

Look what it's done for her cheekbones. Look what it's done for her complexion. Her sadness even smells of citrus. It's not the mink shawl she once found in her grandmother's closet. It's the string of pearls passed down from her mother and her mother's mother and her mother's mother's mother. But, she is no mother. No babies to suckle the sadness. No babies to burp up the sadness. Such pride in her sadness. Such stunning photos of her sadness. They love her sadness. They write, *So gorgeous.* They write, *Beautiful.* They want more. They want more of her sadness. They click a million *likes* for her sadness. They say she looks like Garbo. They say she wears her sadness like a silent film star. They envy her sadness. They starve for her sadness. They post selfies of themselves frowning. Furrow their eyebrows. Drop Artificial Tears in their eyes. They ask, *How can she have no babies? How can the sadness stop here?*

Happy Poem

Point me out the happy man and I will point out either egotism, selfishness, evil—or else absolute ignorance.
—Graham Greene

Growing up I played hide n' seek with happiness
while my father strummed Costello's

Alison I know this world is killin you...Oh Alison...
Happiness is a tricky bastard. I don't think I ever won.

I'm going to be honest: I've had some trouble with happiness.
As a kid, my best friend was a sock puppet named Garbanzo.

In my twenties, I came to the overwhelming conclusion
humans disappoint me. But now, in my thirties,

I've come to the conclusion I disappoint myself—
progress or perhaps I've become more ignorant with age

and maybe by the time I'm fifty I'll reach absolute ignorance.
Maybe happiness will reveal itself, unfold like the truth

eventually did, while my ex was out humping happiness
and asking me, *Why can't you ever write a happy poem?*

I tried but they always smelled like Elmer's Glue and looked
like crumpled moons. My mom named my sister

after Costello's song and would tell her *You create your own hell,*
Allison, but she told me, *You create your own happiness.*

When I Google happiness, a picture of a pig in mud
appears on my computer screen. My sister always wanted a pig.

Perhaps if our mom would have allowed her a pig,
there would have been no discussion of happiness, or hell.

The pig would have been enough.

Actresses: Marie Antoinette Addresses Marilyn

They changed Norma Jean to Marilyn.
They changed my name from Antonia to Marie Antoinette.

Groomed like a poodle
for a dog show, I entered Versailles.
I wore big feathers on my head.
You dyed your hair platinum.
It took you hours of makeup
before you shimmied across the screen.
It took me hours of pulling, pinning, powdering
just to get outside my bedroom door.
They made you gain weight.
They made me have babies.
You yearned to be loved
and I yearned to find love.
She's pretty but dumb
the public said of you.
She's pretty but frivolous
the public said of me.
They conditioned you to play dumb,
provided me with everything to be frivolous.

We both interfered with politics.
You just wanted to get away.
I just wanted to be deported.

I was never The Queen of France.
It was merely a role I played.

Love Song for Bastards

O my dears, all the world's fathers
are playing a concerto of pianos for you—
they're singing their sorry reasons as the moon
spits down her sadness; they're
wearing their fingers down,
a bunch of broken Beethovens—
fingertips bleeding, calloused, a chorus of fathers,
their voices violins out of tune.
Maybe they're singing about the year you were born,
the year Carter took office—Carter, who couldn't
point the big shiny missile, couldn't get elected
another term. Maybe they're singing about
the old woman who approached your mother
and whispered, *You know, she's a bastard*
as the clouds came down and muffled
your ears—or you watched the television's colors,
in awe of the furrowed brows and raspy
voices that spoke of hostages through thick smoke,
or maybe how the woman died years later as Dan Quayle
preached about the nuclear family, her last words
gurgled—*bastards, bastards…*
Perhaps a bastard put her out of her misery,
closed the big brown coffin of her heart.
O my darlings, tonight the stars are Flamenco
dancers, the black sky is a mother's
sleepy voice singing *if that cradle don't break.*
No need to check the stove over and over,
no need to think about the times you'd ask about
him and throats would cackle like fire, their words

fistfuls of hair stuck in a drain. No, open your chests
and let your thousands of sins fly out.
I will catch them, one by one,
and cradle them like newborns.

All I Know of Love

Love has failed me like a politician fails his people.
It's just a realization. The same way I realized,

as a child, like the people of Alexandria once realized,
the stars are not fixed, not just little goblets of gold in the sky.

I think of how my ex remarried two years after I left.
His new wife moved into the apartment we once lived in.

And maybe love is as easily replaced as the politician.
I don't know. All I know of love is this: I once read

about a poisonous fish served in Japan. How even
with the most skilled chef, the diner often ends up

paralyzed, then dead. How they are often almost buried alive
until a mother sees some movement, hears a heartbeat.

This is the City Where I Once Lived

but today my eyes refract all the light
until the street lights are swings and
the cars are not really cars, but cows,
fields of cows, that won't let me pass.
I look them in the eye and they say, *Moo*.
The ocean opens her hand and waves,
the clouds are white sheets on big beds
and the sky is a huge hotel. All these windows—
merely eyes winking. *Good for you*, the stucco says,
Good for you. The palm trees bow their heads
which makes the crows fall from their hair
but they don't yell like they used to.
I am doing just fine. And the ambulances
are voluptuous opera singers singing
Solamente una vez, and our old apartment
is a piece of dust floating away.

Bonnie Without Clyde

Blue as usual.
—Bonnie Parker, 1910—1934

Part One: Delete
No thousands of people crowd
around her dead body, a doll displayed
for the spectators; no one slides
her wedding ring from her swollen
finger; no bullets spray like oil from a well;
no photo flash; no smell of singed skin
that leaves her leg limp; no decision
there will be no trial; no Clyde—Clyde
with his smooth hair, smooth suit and confidence
as big as the Texas sky. No home
of backwater, home of mud
and belly ache, of mother without
enough potatoes to boil, without enough
onion to make her children cry; no
thief she marries at fifteen, no thief
who takes wallets and bread, but leaves
her with bruises as bright as berries
from bushes. No more no—
yes, let's let her father go; it will
put spark in her bones.

Part Two: Stop
A girl sits with pencil and paper, a girl made of skin and bone,
made of hunger, made of strawberry hair and a mind full of places

with more than outhouses and taste of dirt, places with smooth
sidewalk, click of heel. She's heard the comments, the boys from

the city who whisper, *I know what girls from your side will do for a dime*—
their words charcoal, wood. She's heard her mother say she can do
better

by *marrying a lawyer, a banker*. But focus: listen to the squeak of lead
against her notebook, to the sound of clouds moving fast in her head.

She writes, *blue as usual*—the *u* two arms reaching for something new,
for something better than this, for something with sunsets orange as
flame.

    Part Three: Rewrite

Sometimes they show up in my dreams—Clyde,
the other ones from my teens—but I barely
recognize them. They're like mud on my shoe
before I realize it smells of shit. And, I don't think
they'd know what to make of me—of my marriages,
of my degrees, of my poetry. I left at eighteen, left
the rot and sulfur, left my mother's silence with a
head full of Whitman and Frost—of course, no women.
People hissed *poetess*, but it just tasted of tinder,
of dry grass. They warned I'd never make it,
warned I'd go mad and I did, but I also found
Moore, H.D., and Millay. I'm unsure how a woman
doesn't go mad trying to move through this world.
I'm unsure of many things. I'm unsure how I became
someone whose pistol is her poetry, whose words
made her drive away on a blue Texas day, whose
made of crackle, of burn.

For Mud

Mud, wet mess of minerals and muck, when I was a girl
I'd try to dig through, reaching for respite, reaching

for something new. I'd listen, listen for suction, for the sink
of boot. Mud, thirty years later, I still set my hands & fingers

& feet in your grit. Muddy my puritanical roots. Muddy my past loves.
Let them slowly slide into your smooth silt. Let them leave

the mudslide of my mind. Mud, I love the cool stick of you,
love your proteins & trace elements. Swallow my years of trying

to slow down; swallow my desire, my cause of so many sinkholes.
Mud, filthy sucker of soil and slurp, keep me close to dirt.

Close to Earth. Close to dust. Mud, make me stay put.

Notes

The following books greatly helped me learn about, and understand, Catherine the Great, Marie Antoinette, and Cleopatra: *Catherine The Great: Portrait of a Woman*, by Robert K. Massie, *Marie Antoinette: The Last Queen of France*, by Evelyne Lever, and *Cleopatra: A Life*, by Stacy Schiff.

"Marie Antoinette & Sylvia Plath Go for Ice Cream"
The term "bitch goddess" refers to the biographer Edward Butscher, who labeled Plath a "bitch goddess" throughout his biography *Sylvia Plath: Method & Madness*.

"Bonnie Without Clyde"
The epigraph is from Bonnie Parker's diary and was in the PBS special *Bonnie & Clyde*, which inspired this poem.

Chrys Tobey's poems have appeared in *Plough-shares, The Cincinnati Review, New Ohio Review, the minnesota review, Rattle,* and elsewhere. She lives in Portland, Oregon.

CPSIA information can be obtained
at www.ICGtesting.com
Printed in the USA
LVOW06s1435040417
529577LV00029B/368/P